Brain, Heart and Quantum

Poetry Collection
INTO MY GARDEN
Homage to Emily Dickinson

Hector Geager

Brain, Heart and Quantum

Nueva York Poetry Press LLC
128 Madison Avenue, Suite 2RN
New York, NY 10016, USA
+1(929)354-7778
nuevayork.poetrypress@gmail.com
www.nuevayorkpoetrypress.com

Brain, Heart and Quantum
© 2024 Hector Geager

ISBN 13 - 978-1-966772-03-3

© *Into My Garden Collection vol.* 03
(Homage to Emily Dickinson)

© Publisher:
Marisa Russo

© Editor:
Francisco Trejo

© Blurb:
Priscilla y Gustavo Gac-Artigas

© Cover Designer:
William Velásquez Vásquez

© Layout Designer
Moctezuma Rodríguez

© Cover Artist:
Pablo Mejías Chavarría

© Author Photograph:
Author's personal archives

Geager, Hector
Brain, Heart and Quantum / Hector Geager. 1ª ed. New York: Nueva York Poetry Press, 2024, 120 pp. 5.25" x 8".

1. American Poetry.   2. Hispanic American Poetry

All rights reserved. No part of this publication may be reproduced, distributed, or transmitted in any form or by any means, including photocopying, recording, or other electronic or mechanical methods, without the prior written permission of the publisher and the author except in the case of brief quotations embodied in critical reviews and certain other noncommercial uses permitted by copyright law. For permissions contact the publisher at: nuevayork.poetrypress@gmail.com.

THE MAKE BELIEVE

Everything falls some break some don't

like my heart when you dropped it

like the leaves that a vacuum sucked

a floor is a destroyer of fallen glasses cups

and feelings whenever they escape the hands that

    hold them

It's not only time which toasts their nature

and the blueness can't be unbroken

no one wants to be alive shattered pieces on a cold

    floor no shoes

and without seeing it coming

a slippery hand inattentive couldn't read the future

why should you care for falling things . . .

an essential make believes.

IDEAS

What's the evolutionary advantage

of a strange behavior when circling a thought,

such a delicate organism trying to survive,

adapting to the great pressure of deep water.

Submersibles and under air photographies deeper

    dives

into the mind exploring and discovering new

    species of ideas,

feelings and emotions bizarre fascination,

with the never pondered

before the never videotaped curiosity structural

    functionality

odd-looking mental creatures thinly swimming

        around

electrical impulses and chemical reactions

in constant communication make us be.

PERCEPTION

Subjectively blind to the self-changes illusionary

stability balancing acts predictions to predictions

for existing all best guesses in our interaction with

    a may-not-be reality

with the imperative to be alive

and being aware perceptions

that have internal causes we are believing

    our free will

Isn't it a perception, too?

Seeing the world each differently in a universe

of other minds expanding, moving away

from one another riddles of reality incessantly

    going

from quarks to the cosmos

and back to a fragile self an entanglement of space

    and time

Isn't it a perception, too?

You are not who you think you really

are there is not actuality in the word you,

not fixation just changing from one state

of existence to another carbon fourteen

in decay a lucid dream or a sleep meditation

Isn't it a perception, too?

You tell me!

Dissolving

Your life with its natural ecosystem leaving

    footprints

taking memory layers upon layers sandstones

and shellfish looking through a telescope

at primordial galaxies that shouldn't have existed

    before thinking

source of ancient energy pulsating at the edge

    of my universe

sad supernova non existential avoidance turning

into a black hole absorbing lies after lies ready

to explode at any time to create another paralleled

    universe of disbelief

loss star travels through your life aimlessly

while I remain your observation post.

UNKNOWN

An avatar construct of emotional bones extracted

from a cave in the middle of the chest

Cosmic Time Machine breathing in a blue zone

Irreverent… psychological suspense

Outlander traveler, trying to pick myself up

from this epic battle, raunchy melody gruesome

thriller piercing my soul with captivating fury

Drama, rivalry in a sentimental stew

of a still forgotten love loss inside a black mirror in

    a medieval me

Beyond this reality turned into fantasy my sandy

    self-calling

out of his death

With you a never more, I am tempted to go to his

forevermore.

THE MOUSE TRAP

Diverted road

huff and puff

a sense of in directionality

leading to the same point

in a black massive powerful

unknown musketeer with no cannon ball, my lady

Defenseless mental castles

a journey getting brighter, just an illusion,

but felt we were improving the circle

    with new lights

lines in new signaling system

for faster journey in a liquid future like every

    journey mattered

there wasn't cheese dried well

as I kept trying to make a greener journey

      for everyone

a separate reality

bizarre experience stewed because of no

      improvement plan

pure imagination trapped in coconut oil

Never could get you past your breaking point

you, a constancy boiling point

and I ended up asphyxiated in your mousetrap.

A TREE

Deciduous branches mother tree holds an

    umbilical cord

Living in blue indifference leaves

—humans sparkle of toxic air

Airborne chemical particles

venous gas roots of ancestral malandrines

Makes feel like humanity rains

A cup of water with lemon half

a teaspoon of salt and a teaspoon

of sugar we're watery ghosts past love without

    roots

Without trunk

Without fruits

Nothing is nothing

Something is nothing

And the apple falls.

SEPARATION

The drier shrinks my thoughts washed up ideas

anachronistic grinder of diluted dreams

Traveling through spaces going backwards

at different points, different me

At different times going forward ever-increasing distances

separation after a hug—creation of more space

A life may hang from a second light-year that

      I sleep

time chasing time in an all-around desert

of caramelized rapid eye movement

Death is the speed of dark matter moving away

from the Big Bang,

an undoing like a dissolution of iodine in water

Me, imagined dissolution

you, separated reality

we, dissolved Jellybeans

OPPOSITE DIRECTIONS

Time, dissolution of sugar into water

—we are no more

no more constricted space between us

no more relentless independent gravity

no more two hearts dancing radiation

Nebular love hydrogenic formation

no more; the end of our short journey,

a time lapse, a salted blink in a left-unattended look

Wanderers of the universe craving

for new existential episodes to be reborn

in the dynamic of a simple "Hello"

no more.

Disappearance

The missing thought

The thought that never was

That wasn't born

That didn't have a chance to grow

An idea lost

Absence of creation,

genuflexión of words air hollows

of wind no surrounding landscape

or ears altered

No thought to think without even

to know a grandiose smallness,

it disappeared into nothing.

The Try

Uploading a new operating system to be a present

Soporific device my thinking in a sea of dreams,

navigating on a schooner idea upon ideas from past

    to past

Updating me fast-forward to delete all data

that slowed down

my processing speed moving

forward dream boat restful and a deep I

Irresistible, grandly future me.

THE BIG-BREAK

Complex miser ecosystem of broken promises dynamics paces on sea of dreams and spaced memories navigating her pernicious remains, deviated skeletons breath my mind unknown location in a laconic fakeness, in a honeycomb with abnormal formality gentil water dripping my starship thinking about the protagonist in our travel through oceans change forms from navigators to crocodiles to boats to drops of hot ice... until I wake up again and again or sleep from coast to coast on wet eyes, or jump from hope to hope with a jumping rope escaping her spiderwebs.

ANIMAL GOD

Oh! human species in need of editing mental DNA to extract your genetic violence, prejudice and emotional distortions

Oh! Convert yourself into a well-thought-out creature to honor your highest self-stops falling into your abysmal sweet ignorance: paper being

Combine your thinking stew it into reviewing all your beliefs and step out of your comfortable position of medieval okra; become a new, better version of vegetable

Compress your feelings and desires be a humble cracker feed the famine in your head with new words and concepts—you are a failed universal standard for safety, for kindness for fraternity

Update yourself to a time-traveling operating system and cease crashing Microsoft.

PARTICLES

Particles in a miniature life bouncing from hand to

    hand

Dissociative existence

with your inexhaustible impatience perseverant

    being

Reality is just a mere illusion

of your distorted mind akin to atomic

    unpredictability

—persistent illusory thoughts, yet with deliberate

    intention

If a look is a fractal reflection of what we feel,

feelings in you are fatally scorched like iron heated

    to white

Quantum vibrations evils black matter sucking up

all existential lights and thermal heat around you

Eloped in thermodynamics self-love spaceship:

self-steaming away from your minuscule life,

minor atmospheric disturbance.

Us

Infinite number of times

billions and billions of stars and worlds like my
    head
intelligent life forms without communicating
    among each other

Infinite number of out of the body's experiences,

experiencing feelings that float in and out of us

    gaseously

Infinite number of existences; occupying spaces in

    a multiverse:

dying in one universe, yet still living in another

with identical behaviors and patterned similitudes

Do dreams connect all our multiverse parallel

    beings?

Wouldn't night be the connector for all our

    similarities in its darkness?

US.

The Three Body Problem

Is it just a mathematical problem or beyond? Or is it a symbol of the human spirit challenging our existential history? What's really true is it's chaotic nature, the havoc created by its pulling and tossing among any three bodies trying to please their gravitational forces and the tug of war shaping us in constant disharmony unraveling secrets, which threatens our emotionally charged equilibrium; yanking us out of orbits —in a deep connection to an infinite rotation of hurt and reconstruction of the self; so infidelity is not, it's never a triangle— it is a multiplicity of spherical bodies gyrating around one another in desire leading to their eventual total destruction and total awakening: incessantly dying and resurrecting.

QR CODE

Scan it and read the menu of a personality: human nature at its best absence of forces, pull, push, gravity or electromagnetic energy that may lead to psychological malfunctions or inaccuracy; so, there is not randomness in this natural construct in this subatomic level

Scan the QR Code observe the behaviors and notice the patterns in the position and momentum, orientation and angular momentum, its voltage and free electric charge, its electric field and electric polarization density-unfortunately, they cannot be predicted simultaneously appearing to be a mind-bending chaos, yet an orderly mindful mental operation in Quantum mechanics our own particles fields: Our QR

WHY TO WRITE POETRY?

"Why do you write poetry?", she asks me—making fun of me while twisting her lips and further disfiguring her drunk and grotesque face.

In a pensive—like when you miss the mental train—trying to find my conceptual bearing, I asked: "What is a rose for?" "Why a God create a world?" "When is consciousness really conceived in the environmental uterus?"

A shadowy silence overcame her light, then she turned on her ignorance and sheltered herself, amidst her whoring.

I heard the "fuck yourself!" as she exited, muttering— "why do you write poetry?" and I thought, "to fuck myself."

Finding Solitude

Getting a hard on solitude

—the best onboarding experiences

your heart has ever had

—a rippling effect through your body

No impact on anything

No effusiveness

A colorless emotional wave in the vast world

of leaves and train stations opening like iron petals

    of water lilies

Soundless melodic dance awakens the pineal gland

Odorless afternoon remembrances of bygone

    Siestas

—raining silence hollering thinking

Dissolving sunlight shaking as a saltshaker

A silence opens another silence:

one on one; though it's more of a mano a mano

Quiet escapes to under a rug.

CONFUSION

A misleading guide to the true nature of reality

—confusion

my supposed reality is solely mine living in a holographic organ; your reality is yours, unlike mine: interactions among perception, interpretation and
      experiences

in search of consciousness, things can be created

      in empty space

further confusion in everyday situations that we

      can hardly recognize I, you, we

in a constant state of flow our existential becoming within a universe perceived and owned only by each

quantum field remains even in the absence of our

      particles in any space

because a vacuum is low energy, but no zero
    energy—lost in spacetime

particles and antiparticles gravitational and electromagnetic forces interactions in space and time with us, in us in any real sense, space is habitable there isn't maximum nothingness; a Casimir Effect where you attract me and I attract you—two metallic plates of attraction in a vacuum without no pushing, no pulling, spontaneously moving and getting together: confusion or love?

Both!

THE ORDINARY

This is me—perhaps no a good skin care solution

    for everyone—Niacinamide

I may even out your skin tone

And, reduce the impact of your environmental

damage: from childhood to adulthood

I may visibly minimize your life's enlarged pores

Fight dark spots

Improve premature signs of aging, as your thinking

    goes

I may tighten your eyesight; the skin around some

    crazy ideas of mine

And, improve the melody in your skin tone

    —hydrating your existentialist

philosophical protection

I'm not endorsed by a famous celebrity an

influencer or your friend who uses me

I may be of therapeutic benefits, though

And, I can cost you an ordinary amount—nothing

Really, nothing ordinary.

Tin Heart

An octagon-shaped heart jukebox reduced to half, then to half—doesn't function in a continues scale, like a microscopic universe it functions at discreet quantities—you human string guitar of uncertainty principle: why? oh, typical manifestation of evil long nails that heart in a bottle of disguised courage: pretender.

I reduce criticality to your minimal expression, a trip home—forest of planted soldiers rifle flowers of legal killing brainless, heartless telescopic bullets—historical ignorance cubic massacres; I don't fight, caught in limbo.

WE ARE NOT REAL

Infinitesimal cauldron combination and recombination in our unreal reality, which is holographic a mere illusion a nothingness fiction of a physical reality in constant movement our bosons having consciousness of themselves changing when looking at their alteration platitude—how do they know that we observe them? do the observable observe us too? we—reductionists—search for the smallest particles of matter outside ourselves building blocs of life spacetime measure of uncertainty in a system information hologram are we all empty yellow butterflies false perception interpreted in our brains and influenced by our surrounding reality is real only when we see it but each one with an own reality so to cling to the measurable and observable encircling our particular thoughts about what it is and what it isn't.

EXISTING

$WE = O2 + H2O$

Quest congratulatory lyrics, desperately hoping ET

    origins where all is biological luck

happenstance among trillion of possibilities to

create and us of useable genetic combinations

pollution-generating flesh and bones machines

exhibiting that proud ignorance that is solely

    of ours

after so much science still fear of the unknown

    keeping gods and fairy godmothers alive

what's your fear mental midget?

what's your security none-fullness entity?

why don't you . . .

and me, embrace our thoughts—bosoms

of Gibbs—gibberish changing when looked at

may be, those bosoms are the ever-elusive souls.

DISAPPOINTMENT

Mindless descontructing the mind of its mindset in a finite groundbreaking insistence on the rational

Concepts and principles to think through life's experiences dogmas beliefs searching in constant revision

Demolition ball hitting again and again egocentric ideas smashing and building a new selfless self devoid of community thinking—expulsions of socio-centric thought to be more humane

Freeing the mind from its foggy surroundings slavery of cognitive and social biases framework trapping these existential issues while continuously approaching through a motherly looking glass

Opening doors of common and uncommon denominator inconsistencies windows peering into prejudices in infinite numbers thought—provoking causes in a constant justification of human existence—disappointments sea

Still navigating

26 CATHEDRAL MAN

The glow within an idea

An ideal walking ahead

ahead of the sublime inert at first

A glowing heartbeat in a separation of reality

Outrunning vibrations flying papers watery

    fireflies

Cerebral sugarcane properly dragging creative

    vibes crustacean waves

Irreverent specificity separates the relevant from

    the irrelevant caducity

Torpedoes the irrational: what's the essential

    question?

Photo gallery courtesy of words and cogitation

Glow wishing burst out inkling soul

Harmonious silence daily anagrams see the

    cathedral man shining

Wrapped in his halo—forest in perennial spring

Cathedral man an ideal growing flowering

    each year.

WE ARE HERE

Stream chain of filaments unknown nothingness

 —does our universe have a purpose?

Neutrons passing and changing personalities space

 spawning dark matter

Mind-blowing nothing is realistically real time

 jumping consciousness

Scary quantum reality as we are everything and

 nothing water and neurons

All that is in one's own mind no matter who's

 the observer and who created

Yet… we are here.

COLD SPACE

From ice floe to ice floe—can the wind survive the

    ice pressure?

Ice cycles dancing burning us firewood from fire

    to fire: under the blanket our sweat tires

Cold feet quest for warmth frosting one another

open heart surgery memory follows memory

A Memorial Day weekend for hands over our past

    devoid of eyesight frozen rain lost paper

Like snake curled in the mouth a sidereal mountain

    range snow elopes with sidewalk

A light expands gelid breezes tears on the walls a

    pensive blizzard blinks by my eyes

We are not longer we.

LEMON WOMAN

Fumbling her way through intense tears darkened

    Christmas' death loneliness

Searching scary houses in mindfulness, for past

    ghosts and dancing goblins

Her transformational neurons traveling on beam

    of lights revering in lemon juice

Smoke-filled life: no purpose in sight no

    visualization dark imagery teary eyes

Neurosis without gaps trapped under collapsed

    roof in fires after fires crystalline cries

Wasted in traumas toxic trunks toxic bus-stopped

    on December 12

Wonder lemon woman rarely sugar rarely found taste.

GRASSHOPPER

Seeing over your glasses beyond its gravitational

force into the universal creation of a supernova

—lost grasshopper

Microscopic feelings so you always say—and who

believes you when jumping from a field to reach

    the moon grasshopper?

Deceiving sunlight magnetic waves—in constant

portraying of a who you are not grasshopper

Masquerading distorted self jump to spins stories:

    you never played violin grasshopper

Strings of neutrinos men plus more men atoms

then molecule formation—you have not home

    grasshopper

Grasshopper you are gas

Grasshopper you are air

In a symphony music is green in another concert

      brown

Grasshopper you are not liquid

Grasshopper you are not solid

Jello's character like a weasel's but… fortunately,

      you don't speak English.

REMEMBRANCE

A memory of sorrow needs a camera

two particles colliding in empty space creating something from nothing: sometimes anti-particles in an incessant tree of we frozen images in paired
    movement

At the subatomic level we are not separated entities, although traumas divide our mison's quark
    from its antiquark

Two antiparticles' pairs extracted of the space birthed by our antiquark: still a strong electromagnetic attraction field between us, or just me? Is it that the unending origin of our emotional being?
A limbic love surging from a vacuum itself where there was nothing: emptiness without particles or anti-particles dance floor idealization previous be
    lief in highest energy

We were an experiment gone wrong; the total failure of a romantic system in extreme unreal astrophysical environments of arguably cosmic strength personality fields, like filming our feelings
    and desires.

ABOUT THE AUTHOR

Hector Geager es escritor y profesor de Educación y Liderazgo. Ha ayudado a organizaciones a desarrollar e implementar sistemas internos de rendición de cuentas, implementar y gestionar el cambio en las organizaciones y establecer equipos de alto rendimiento a nivel empresarial. Formador de numerosos profesionales que construyen grandes equipos de negocios, al comprender cómo darse cuenta del papel del trabajo en equipo y la colaboración para lograr un alto rendimiento del personal a nivel organizacional. Algunos de sus premios y reconocimientos son: el Intelectual Fulbright 2009, el Premio SIMA Global Ambassadors Humanitarian action Award 2021, el Premio SIMA Global Leader of Year 2022, el The President of the United States' Life Time Achievement Award 2022 y el Doctorado Honoris y Causa, Madrid, España 2022. Es autor de los libros de poesía *El Subway, 30 poemas y una bachata, September Blue Jays, Como la muerte de una vela, Murmullos del observador* y *El Rey de la Muerte*.

TABLE OF CONTENTS

Brain, Heart and Quantum

The Make Believe ·	11
Ideas ·	15
Perception ·	19
Dissolving ·	23
Unknown ·	27
The Mouse Trap ·	31
A Tree ·	35
Separation ·	39
Opposite Directions ·	43
Disappearance ·	45
The Try ·	47
The Big-Break ·	49
Animal God ·	51
Particles ·	53
US ·	57
The Three Body Problem ·	61
QR Code ·	63
Why to Write Poetry? ·	65
Finding Solitude ·	67
Confusion ·	71
The Ordinary ·	75
Tin Heart ·	79
We are not real ·	81
Existing ·	83
Disappointment ·	87

26 Cathedral Man · 89
We Are Here · 93
Cold Space · 95
Lemon Woman · 97
Grasshopper · 99
Remembrance · 103

About the Author · 107

INTO MY GARDEN
COLLECTION

English Poetry
Homage to Emily Dickinson

1
September Blue Jays
Hector Geager

2
Embroidered Colony of Love
María Palitachi

2
Brain, Heart and Quantum
Hector Geager

Poetry Collections

Adjoining Wall
Pared Contigua
Spaniard Poetry
Homage to María Victoria Atencia (Spain)

Barracks
Cuartel
Poetry Awards
Homage to Clemencia Tariffa (Colombia)

Crossing Waters
Cruzando el Agua
Poetry in Translation (English to Spanish)
Homage to Sylvia Plath (United States)

Dream Eve
Víspera del Sueño
Hispanic American Poetry in USA
Homage to Aida Cartagena Portalatin (Dominican Republic)

Fire's Journey
Tránsito de Fuego
Central American and Mexican Poetry
Homage to Eunice Odio (Costa Rica)

Into My Garden
English Poetry
Homage to Emily Dickinson (United States)

I Survive
Sobrevivo
Social Poetry
Homage to Claribel Alegría (Nicaragua)

LIPS ON FIRE
LABIOS EN LLAMAS
Opera Prima
Homage to Lydia Dávila (Ecuador)

LIVE FIRE
VIVO FUEGO
Essential Ibero American Poetry
Homage to Concha Urquiza (Mexico)

FEVERISH MEMORY
MEMORIA DE LA FIEBRE
Feminist Poetry
Homage to Carilda Oliver Labra (Cuba)

REVERSE KINGDOM
REINO DEL REVÉS
Children's Poetry
Homage to María Elena Walsh (Argentina)

STONE OF MADNESS
PIEDRA DE LA LOCURA
Personal Anthologies
Homage to Julia de Burgos (Argentina)

TWENTY FURROWS
VEINTE SURCOS
Collective Works
Homage to Julia de Burgos (Puerto Rico)

WILD MUSEUM
MUSEO SALVAJE
Latin American Poetry
Homage to Olga Orozco (Argentina)

OTHER COLLECTIONS

Fiction
INCENDIARY
INCENDIARIO
Homage to Beatriz Guido (Argentina)

Children's Fiction
KNITTING THE ROUND
TEJER LA RONDA
Homage to Gabriela Mistral (Chile)

Drama
MOVING
MUDANZA
Homage to Elena Garro (Mexico)

Essay
SOUTH
SUR
Homage to Victoria Ocampo (Argentina)

Non-Fiction/Other Discourses
BREAK-UP
DESARTICULACIONES
Homage to Sylvia Molloy (Argentina)

For those who think as Emily Dickinson, that: *There is another sky, ever serene and fair, and there is another sunshine, though it be darkness there.* **Brain, Heart and Quantum** by Hector Geager invites you to come *Into [her] garden*. This book was published in April 2025 by Nueva York Poetry Press in the United States of America

Made in the USA
Middletown, DE
30 June 2025